Every Kid's Guide to
Being Special

Written by
JOY BERRY

CHILDRENS PRESS ®
CHICAGO

About the Author and Publisher

Joy Berry's mission in life is to help families cope with everyday problems and to help children become competent, responsible, happy individuals. To achieve her goal, she has written over two hundred self-help books for children from birth through age twelve. Her work revolutionized children's publishing by providing families with practical, how-to, living skills information that was previously unavailable in children's books.

Joy gathered a dedicated team of experts, including psychologists, educators, child developmentalists, writers, editors, designers, and artists, to form her publishing company and to help produce her work.

The company, Living Skills Press, produces thoroughly researched books and audio-visual materials that successfully combine humor and education to teach subjects ranging from how to clean a bedroom to how to resolve problems and get along with other people.

Managing Editor: Ellen Klarberg
Copy Editor: Kate Dickey
Contributing Editors: Libby Byers, Nancy Cochran, Maureen Dryden,
Yona Flemming, Kathleen Mohr, Susan Motycka
Editorial Assistant: Sandy Passarino

Art Director: Laurie Westdahl
Design: Abigail Johnston, Laurie Westdahl
Production: Abigail Johnston, Caroline Rennard
Illustrations designed by: Bartholomew
Inker: Susie Hornig
Colorer: Susie Hornig
Composition: Curt Chelin

Do you know that you are a special person?

In **EVERY KID'S GUIDE TO BEING SPECIAL** you will learn the following:

- every person is special,
- you have a one-of-a-kind body,
- you have a one-of-a-kind personality,
- you have a one-of-a-kind situation,
- you are one-of-a-kind,
- your body is all right,
- your emotions are all right,
- not being perfect is all right, and
- you are a special person.

Every person is special.

Even though this is true, there are some people who do not feel special because

- they do not feel valuable or
- they feel bad about themselves.

It is important for you to feel good about yourself so you can be happy and accomplish all that you were born to accomplish.

In order to feel good about yourself, you must
- realize that you are a valuable person and
- understand and accept everything about being a person.

You have a one-of-a-kind *body.*
No other person has a body exactly the same size
and shape as your body.

You have a *face* that does not look like any other person's face.

You have **teeth** that are not exactly like any other person's teeth.

No other person has *hair* exactly like your hair.

You have **hand, finger,** and **foot prints** that are not like any other person's prints.

No other person has a *body odor* that smells exactly like your body odor.

In addition to a one-of-a-kind body, you have a one-of-a-kind *personality.*

Your personality is made up of many personal traits.

What you like is a personal trait.

Another personal trait is *what interests you.*

What you believe is a personal trait.

Another personal trait is *what makes you laugh.*

How you show your feelings is a personal trait.

Another personal trait is *how you feel and act around people.*

What you do well and do not do well are personal traits.

Other personal traits are *your good and bad habits.*

Whether or not you do what you say you will do is a personal trait.

Another personal trait is *whether or not you like to work hard.*

Whether you are neat or messy is a personal trait.

Another personal trait is *whether you do things quickly or slowly.*

All of your personal traits make up your personality.

No other person has a personality exactly like yours.

No other person has a combination of personal traits exactly like yours.

In addition to a one-of-a-kind body and a one-of-a-kind personality, you have a one-of-a-kind *situation*.

The people in your life help create your situation. Some of the people in your life are

- your family and relatives,
- your friends,
- the people you do not get along with, and
- any other people you relate to.

The places in your life also help create your situation. Some of the places in your life are

- your home,
- your school,
- your church or temple (if you attend one),
- where you play, and
- where you work (if you work).

The possessions in your life help create your situation. Your possessions are the things you own.

Your experiences also help create your situation.
Your experiences are

- what you do,
- the good things that happen to you, and
- the bad things that happen to you.

No other person has a situation exactly like yours.

Everything that surrounds and involves you creates your situation.

You have a one-of-a-kind
- body,
- personality, and
- situation.

This makes you a one-of-a-kind person.

Because you are a one-of-a-kind person, you are not like any other person in the world.

No one can replace you.
Because you cannot be replaced, you are valuable.

Even though you are one-of-a-kind, there might be some things you do not like about yourself. However, to feel good about yourself, you should realize that you are acceptable because you are a person. Because you are a person, *you have a body that does things that might seem strange or embarrassing.*

There are times when you might need to
- go to the bathroom,
- vomit,
- hiccup,
- sneeze,
- burp, or
- pass gas.

You might also

- snore when you sleep or
- have a stomach that makes rumbling sounds when you are hungry.

You do not need to be embarrassed or feel bad about anything your body does.

Every person has a body that does things that are strange or embarrassing. These are things the human body does to keep the person alive, well, and comfortable.

Because you are a person, *you will at times experience emotions that cause you to feel strange or uncomfortable.*

There are times when you might feel
- fearful (frightened or scared),
- anxious (worried or nervous),
- frustrated (irritated and discouraged),
- defeated (beaten),
- humiliated (embarrassed or foolish), or
- guilty (as if you had done something wrong).

You might also feel
- grieved (sad),
- disappointed (let down),
- rejected (unwanted),
- lonely (all alone),
- jealous (envious), or
- angry (bad-tempered).

You do not need to be embarrassed or feel bad about experiencing uncomfortable emotions.

Every person experiences uncomfortable feelings at one time or another.

Uncomfortable feelings can cause good things to happen. They can cause a person to
- want to do what needs to be done,
- grow and change for the better, and
- notice and appreciate comfortable feelings.

Because you are a person, *you will at times have accidents.*

You do not need to be embarrassed or feel bad
about having accidents.

No one is perfect.
Everyone has accidents.
Accidents can cause a person to
- slow down and
- be more careful.

Because you are a person, *you will at times make mistakes.*

You do not need to be embarrassed or feel bad about making mistakes.

No one is perfect.
Everyone makes mistakes.
Mistakes can cause a person to learn what is the right and the wrong thing to do.

Because you are a person, *you will at times make wrong choices.*

You do not need to be embarrassed or feel bad
about making wrong choices.

No one is perfect.
Everyone makes wrong choices.
Wrong choices can have a positive effect on your life.
They can teach you to slow down and think more
carefully before you make another choice.

You are a person who
- has a body that does things that might seem strange or embarrassing,
- experiences uncomfortable emotions,
- has accidents,
- makes mistakes, and
- makes wrong choices.

In these ways, you are like every other person.

No one is perfect.

People should not feel bad because they are not perfect.

You should not feel bad either.

Learn to accept yourself.

You are valuable, and you are acceptable.

This makes you a special person!